MW01136189

Rhymes
for

poems children can enjoy
by

tom catalano

to gaetano

FIRST EDITION
Copyright © 2000 by Thomas E. Catalano

Note: Many poems in *Rhymes For Kids!* appeared previously in *Rhyme & Reason, Poetry 'N Motion,* and *Verse Things First* all by **tom catalano**.

Printed in the United States of America

ISBN 1-882646-05-3

Published by:
Wordsmith Books, P.O. Box 361, Morton, IL 61550

CONTENTS

Bubble Trouble

If I want to have some fun

I always chew some bubble gum.

Blow it, blow it, oh so round

until it lifts me off the ground.

And lifts me up above the trees

and carries me along the breeze.

Until I'm so high in the sky

all the birds just fly on by.

How much higher can I go?

All the clouds are down below.

I can hardly see the cars

and I can almost touch the stars.

Suddenly my trip has stopped —

because my bubble gum has popped.

Here I sit with my disgrace

with all this gum upon my face!

tom catalano © 1994

I Wish I Was A Pizza

When I grow up I wish that I

would turn into a pizza pie.

Tomato sauce and lots of cheese

and sausage that is sure to please.

Some people would come near and far

if I was a candy bar.

I would be so nice and sweet,

someone who you'd love to meet.

I'd only wish to have some fun

as a burger on a bun.

Add tomatoes and some cheese,

you'll want to give my bun a squeeze.

Or maybe as a nice surprise

I can be some hot french fries.

• • •

Make me curly, make me straight,

add some catsup, I'd be great.

I think these foods I wish to be

have had a strange effect on me.

Maybe what I *really* wish

is to have some lunch upon my dish!

Eye See

I ride a purple pony,

I caught an orange fish,

I've eaten green spaghetti

that's moving on my dish.

My cat has yellow stripes,

my dog has fur of blue,

something doesn't look quite right

do they look right to *you*?

Maybe all these funny things

would seem to be correct,

if the stripes and dots I see

are 'cause my eyes got checked!

tom catalano © 1994

Little Fishy

Little fishy in the brook

look out for that nasty hook!

While you swim around and play

there are anglers out today.

They'll offer down a little snack

— go for it, you won't be back.

When you see them just stay still

or they'll yank you by the gill.

Remember this down in your pool

— that isn't why you went to school!

tom catalano © 1987

An Elephant Nose

An elephant nose
   as long as my arm.
A nice wooly coat
   like the sheep on a farm.

Eyes like an eagle,
   and ears like a cat.
How great it would be
   if I was like *that*.

A tail like a monkey
   to hang from the trees.
Wings like a butterfly
   to float on the breeze.

                    • • •

Though I might look odd
and a little bit weird,
there's *one* thing for sure
— I'd sure be prepared!

tom catalano © 1999

Hear Today, Gone Tomorrow

What's that you say?
I can not hear.
I can not hear
out of one ear!

I had a cold
up in my head.
It's settled in
my ear instead.

It may go next
into my eyes,
now that would be
a big surprise!

• • •

It may even
go in my hair.
I don't know...
do colds go there?

Where it's headed
heaven knows.
I hope it goes
back to my nose!

tom catalano © 1996

All God's Critters

Those lovely little critters

on walls and on the rugs,

yes they are annoying...

that's why they call them bugs.

They may not look like *we* do

but they still are all God's creatures.

Yet who can trust those crawly things

after watching 'Creature Features'?

I don't suggest you make them friends

or treat them to a meal,

just don't be quick to take your foot

and crush them with your heel.

• • •

Be kind to critters big and small

or some day you will pay,

someone who thinks you're bugging *them*

may step on *you* one day!

tom catalano © 1985

Cute Little Birdie

Little birdie in the tree

you sing your song most constantly.

I don't doubt you try to speak

but would you please just shut your beak?

You can fly — so, big deal

a juicy worm is *your* big meal.

You don't have ears, you don't have toes,

you can't even pick your nose!

I'll tell you of my fantasy:

I'd like to climb up in the tree

and as you eat those crumbs of bread

I'd take a poop upon *your* head!

tom catalano © 1988

The Toy

I've sat on this shelf
for so long that I'm sad.
Once *I* was the toy
that they *had* to have.

The kids would all come
and they'd all stand in line.
The clerk would shout out,
"Okay, one at a time!"

The other toys hoped
that they'd be the one
getting pulled from the shelf
heading home for some fun.

• • •

Yes, those were the days
now I've got the blues
'cuz who wants a toy
that's yesterday's news?

As I collect dust
with each passing day
I wish that someone
would take me away.

I heard the clerk say
that they'd have to make room
if somebody doesn't
come take me home soon.

When all of a sudden
well what should I see
but a cute little child
come walking toward me.

• • •

"There it is, Mama
I knew it'd be here!
It's the one that I wanted,
remember? Last year!"

She hugged me so tight
I thought I would moan,
but I didn't care,
now I had a home.

tom catalano © 1998

A Child's Christmas

I woke one day and chanced to see
the living room had grown a tree!
As if that was not strange enough
Mom and Dad kept adding stuff.
Like colored balls and lots of lights,
and shiny rope that twinkled bright.
Beneath the tree they put a house
with people smaller than a mouse.
Some of them were on one knee
— one was a baby just like me.
Baby Jesus was his name,
and as my parents would explain,
that every year on Christmas morn
we celebrate that He was born.

. . .

We give gifts and drink a toast
with people who we love the most.
So on your birthday I will say,
"Jesus, have a happy day!"

tom catalano © 1991

Christmas Rap

There's a fat old dude
    with the name of Claus
who looks like he's been feeding
    on spaghetti sauce.

He goes around
    every year
giving out presents
    and Christmas cheer.

He's got these dudes
    in a factory
making all the toys
    for under the tree.

Somehow he knows
    if you've been bad or good
and then he comes around
    to your neighborhood.

• • •

He flies around
in a sleigh of red
and everyone remembers
what that fat man said.

He said, "Ho, ho, ho,
and a bottle of rum."
Oh, wait a minute now
that was a different one!

When he gets through
he goes back home
he always likes to write himself
a Christmas poem.

His eye would wink
and his finger snap,
he'd write a poem like this
and call it CHRISTMAS RAP!

tom catalano © 1990

23

A Martian Christmas

It may be hard to understand

exactly what I say,

but once a year we celebrate

our Savior on this day.

We decorate our triblig

with tinz and ornimoes,

and buy each other prezzies

and wrap them in brombows.

We sing our favorite holiwogs

and hang our sashyroos

with hopes by the next morning

they're filled by Sandy Clues.

So in this special season

you may very likely hear:

"Have a Martian Christmas

and a Happy Martian Year!"

tom catalano © 1984

Christmas Spirit

I can still recall
    just like it's yesterday,
the story Grandpa told
    and here is what he'd say.

"I heard a noise outside,
    not knowing what it was,
I had to go investigate
    because...well, just because.

It might have been a thief
    perhaps a wild foe.
In either case I knew
    outside I'd have to go.

• • •

There's nothing in the yard,

as far as I can see.

Still, I felt that something

was staring down at me.

'Can you please lend a hand?'

a voice above me said.

'I meant to hit the roof

but landed here instead.'

Sure enough, above me,

as high as I could see,

sat a little person

on the branches of my tree.

Before I had a chance to

find out what it's about,

the person on that branch

to me began to shout.

• • •

'This is just so typical!

I just can't get it right.

No wonder Santa doesn't

take me on his flight!

I *can't* make toys or wrap them

— I'm not like all the rest.

All the elves have talent

— man, I'm so depressed.'

This just can't be real.

An elf up in my tree?

And that you work for Santa,

that's what you're telling me?

'That's right, I am an elf,

and I'm on Santa's crew.

We've all got assignments

of what we need to do.

• • •

There's Marketing and Research

and all of the toy makers.

There's housekeeping and maintenance

and all the goodie bakers.

There's *so* many jobs to do,

as you can plainly see.

So many more important

than the job they gave to me.

I have to do PR,

some elves just won't get near it.

I have to pump up people

with the Christmas spirit.

Do you know what I mean?

Can you hear what I said?

I'm in charge of morale

in a job that I dread!

• • •

I thought that if I practiced
        I *could* do something else,
and I could be more valuable
        as one of Santa's elves.

I thought that I would try my hand
        at Home Delivery.
But I even messed *that* up
        and now I'm in a *tree*!

I know that it sounds bad,
        or that I am a snob,
but you don't know what it's like
        to have the worst elf job.'

You don't know what you're saying,
        your job it is the best.
Without the Christmas spirit
        forget about the rest!

• • •

Who cares about the presents

and all those other things?

Who cares about the toys

that Santa always brings?

The thing that's most important,

of this there is no doubt,

is joy and love and sharing

— what Christmas is about.

He thought of this a moment,

then said, 'Of course you're right.

I might as well come down,

I can't stay here all night!'

As he started coming down,

he tripped upon a limb.

And he would have fallen

— *if* I hadn't caught him.

• • •

He ran off thanking Grandpa,

   although he couldn't hear it.

But that's the night that Grandpa said

   he caught the Christmas spirit.

tom catalano © 1999

Poor Lonesome Louie

My friends think I'm crazy.

They think that I'm screwy.

And some of them call me

Poor Lonesome Louie.

I prefer quiet

and I don't like noise.

I don't like games,

TV, or toys.

Pipe down all you cars,

you dogs, and you cats!

Keep quiet you kids

with your balls and your bats!

• • •

The talking and talking
and talking all day,
just makes me want to
stand up and say:

It doesn't seem
such a difficult task,
would you all just shut up
— is that too much to ask?

"Poor Lonesome Louie,"
they all like to say.
"He just doesn't like
the games that we play."

It isn't the games
it's the noises they make.
It isn't the games,
make *no* mistake!

• • •

The tings and the pings
and the clippity-clop,
the mush and the smush
and the hippity-hop.

Even the sound of
shuffling feet,
that shuffle along
the shuffling street.

Even the birds
that chirp in the tree
are wasting their chirp
on someone like me.

There's one thing to do
as I'm sure you're aware,
I must get away
from those noises out there!

• • •

I closed all my windows
and closed all my doors.
I stopped doing housework,
I stopped doing chores.

Off went the radio,
off went TV.
Off went the noises
that keep bugging me.

But it didn't stop
the noises, alas.
Somebody outside
was mowing the grass!

"Poor Lonesome Louie,"
I heard them all say.
As I jumped on my bike
and peddled away.

• • •

I rode to the woods,
I was hoping to find
some peace and quiet
and some peace of mind.

There's cheeping and chirping
and crunching of leaves.
There's wind blowing through
the branches of trees.

The woods wasn't for me
I quickly could see.
I had to go somewhere
there wasn't a tree.

I rode to the beach
but the waves and their splash
was constant noise
of crash upon crash.

• • •

I jumped in a rocket

and went to the moon.

I hated the noise

when the rocket went BOOM.

"Poor Lonesome Louie,"

I'd bet they'd all say.

"Found what he wanted

by going away."

No sound did I hear

as I sat on the moon.

I sat there all April,

all May, and all June.

I never heard cars,

no dogs, and no cats.

I never heard kids

with balls or with bats.

• • •

I never heard games
or TV or toys.
I never heard any
particular noise.

What a wonderful silence
and quiet, I say!
It's just what I wanted
all night and all day!

I've got all the quiet
that I can afford.
But now that I do,
well, frankly, I'm bored!

I hate to admit it
but I kind of miss
some everyday sounds
like the sound of Mom's kiss.

• • •

I wish I could hear

all my friends call me screwy.

I wish I could hear them

say "Poor Lonesome Louie."

I want to hear cars,

and dogs, and some cats.

I want to hear kids

with balls and with bats.

If there's *one* thing

I've learned while alone...

I miss the noises that

remind me of home!

tom catalano © 1999

My Friend Mary-Jean

Mary-Jean Pearls

had hair full of curls

    and was just as sweet as can be.

She moved from the city,

but oh what a pity,

    she had just one friend — that was me.

And this is the way

it happened that day

    that I had first met Mary-Jean.

The first day of school

she didn't seem "cool"

    the most nervous kid I had seen.

• • •

She rode the school bus

and was looking at us

    and *not* knowing what she should say.

But no one said, "hi,"

and feeling quite shy,

    she wished she could just go away.

She just didn't dress

like us, and I guess,

    we felt that she didn't fit in.

As hard as she'd try

she couldn't deny

    she didn't know where to begin.

She'd eat all alone

and then she'd go home

    sitting alone on the bus.

She seemed kind of sad

and it was too bad

    'cuz she wasn't much different from us.

• • •

I sat by her side

the rest of the ride

and asked her where she had come from.

She said, "Here and there."

She'd lived everywhere

but now her moving was done.

She said that her dad,

with the job that he had,

meant always moving away.

Her dad settled down

in our little town

and this is the place they will stay.

She said there's no doubt

that moving about

is better when it finally ends.

She started to say,

as she turned away,

"The worst part is I have no friends."

• • •

Mary-Jean Pearls

had hair full of curls

 and was just as sweet as can be.

For once she could say

that *here* she would stay

 and she now had a friend — that was me.

tom catalano © 2000

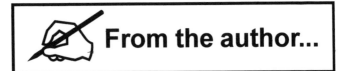

From the author...

"I hope you liked reading my poems. I had fun writing them.

Poetry helps us express ourselves in different ways. I like to write poems that are silly, but I also enjoy writing poems that tell a story about things that are important to me.

Writing poetry is much like having a best friend to talk to. Try it. Think of something you like to do and 'talk' about it in a poem. You'll be glad you did. And you can share that conversation with your 'best friend' every time you read it.

Who knows, maybe someday I'll be reading _your_ poems in a book!"

tom catalano

Acknowledgments

The following people deserve a humongous "THANK YOU" for their help with this book:

Anna Catalano for the idea of the photo layout.

Bob Muntz for staging and taking the photo.

Anna and **Emma Catalano** for starring in the photo... and making me look good!
